Okay, God, so far today I've been squeaky clean.

I haven't lied, cheated, stolen anything --

-- or lusted after Derek.

But now I gotta get up and go to school --

THE ANGRY DEAD

-- so I'm gonna need a **WHOLE** lotta help!

WORST-BRAT FLEES FROM BORG-BOY ACROSS THE ROOFTOPS, UNAWARE OF LOOSE BRICKS BELOW HER FEET!

YOU'LL NEVER CATCH ME ON THESE ROOFTOPS, BORG-BOY!

GASP! WORST-BRAT ISN'T AWARE THOSE BRICKS ARE LOOSE!

SUDDENLY, WORST-BRAT FALLS!

THOSE LOOSE BRICKS!

AIEEE!

I'M FALL-ING!

BORG-BOY USES HIS TELESCOPING ARM TO SAVE WORST-BRAT!

MUST USE MY TELESCOPING ARM TO SAVE WORST-BRAT!

GASP! BORG-BOY SAVED ME WITH HIS TELESCOPING ARM!

PUZZLED, WORST-BRAT ASKS BORG-BOY WHY HE SAVED HER!

YOU SAVED ME, BORG-BOY! WHY?

I HAVE MY REASONS, WORST-BRAT!

Eddie's sweet, but I hope he doesn't expect me to be much company tonight...

God, I am so confused. I need time to think!

Want some pop corn?

Eddie, it's cool...

TEXAS JOE BOB

"It's cool..." That must mean...it's cool!

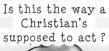

Is this the way a Christian's supposed to act?

It's not a sin to think about it!

But at the same time I'm surfing all kinds of raunchy sites...

Same here. I'm trying to live pure, I wanna live pure...

I feel like I'm betraying everybody in the Prayer Club.

Ditto. I feel so ashamed... so lonely... so frightened.

You?
But I thought Christians didn't feel that way!

Guess again.
Even the best of us have our bad days... or nights.

To be honest, I was hoping this would be a "bad" night...

Last year it woulda been. Sorry, Eddie.

Hey, uh, I'm not trying to embarrass you, but...

...was I gonna be your first?

No.
When I was eleven my sitter thought it would be "cute" if she initiated me.

I've been obsessed with sex ever since.

Thanks. Talking tonight really meant a lot to me.

See ya Monday.

Squeak, thump. Squeak, thump.
Squeak, thump. Squeak, thump.
Squeak, thump. Squeak, splat.

"Squeak, thump.
Squeak, splat ?"

A mouse
failing to
outrun a
bowling
ball down
a flight of
stairs.

Eeeeeeeeeeeeeeeeeeeeeeeee!!!

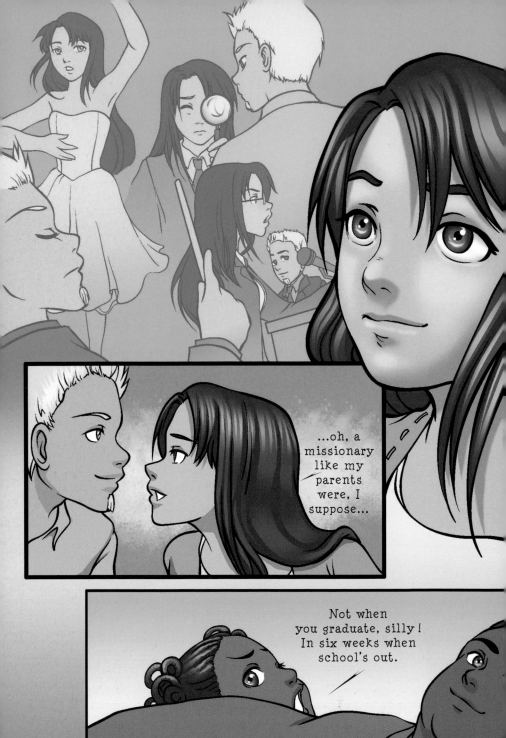

What was **that** ?!?!?

Just the Harper girl yelling.

How can I tell what's right if everybody has a different opinion ?

Sometimes I don't know what to believe.

It's all so confusing !

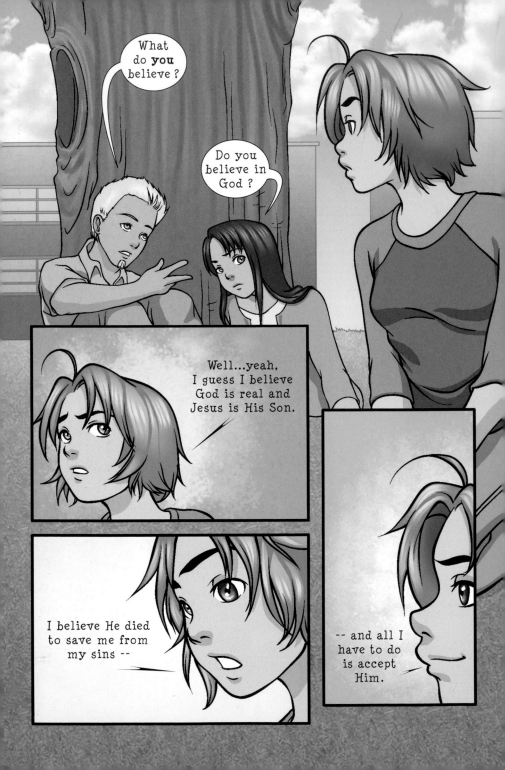

Esther
Queen Of Persia

starring

Serenity
Harper
as
Esther

Derek
Angstrom
as
Xerxes

And A Cast Of Dozens!

Written.Produced.Directed
by
Tim Patterson

GOD SPARED DANIEL AND THE FAITHFUL--

--AND LET PERSIA CONQUER BABYLON.

MANY WENT BACK TO REBUILD JERUSALEM--

SHE WHAT!?!

WHAT IS TO BE DONE WITH A DISOBEDIANT QUEEN?

QUEEN VASHTI WRONGS THE KING AND HIS PEOPLE.

SHE CAUSES DISRESPECT AND DISCORD WITH HER ACTIONS.

IF SHE IS ALLOWED TO IGNORE THE KING, ALL WOMEN WILL LEARN TO DESPISE THEIR HUSBANDS!

BY ROYAL DECREE WHICH CAN NOT BE REPEALED--

--KING XERXES HEREBY FOREVER EXILES QUEEN VASHTI!

LET A SEARCH BE MADE FOR BEAUTIFUL YOUNG VIRGINS--

--THAT SHE WHO PLEASES XERXES BE MADE THE NEW QUEEN.

KING XERXES HAS EXILED QUEEN VASHTI.

HE NOW COMMANDS THE MOST BEAUTIFUL YOUNG VIRGINS IN THE KINGDOM BE BROUGHT TO HIM--

--ALL OF THEM.

COUSIN MORDECAI, YOU LOOK WORRIED. IS SOMETHING WRONG?

HE SEEKS TO REPLACE HER AS QUEEN. YOU'LL HAVE TO--

BUT I CAN'T! I CAN'T MARRY OUTSIDE OUR PEOPLE!

IT WOULD BREAK OUR COVENANT WITH GOD!

ESTHER, AFTER YOUR MOTHER AND FATHER DIED, I HAVE RAISED YOU AS MY OWN DAUGHTER.

???

YOU SHOULD BE HAPPY TO BE HERE.

THROUGH THERE ARE YOUR SLEEPING CHAMBERS, LADIES--

YOU WILL LIVE HERE AND PREPARE UNTIL GREAT XERXES CALLS FOR YOU--

"REQUIRE NOTHING?!?!?" WHAT'S YOUR GAME?

I NEED NOTHING MORE THAN I ALREADY HAVE, SIR. THANK YOU.

WHAT, NO GOLD, JEWELS, OR FINE SILK?

I REQUIRE NONE OF THAT, THANK YOU.

JUST HEALTHY FOOD TO EAT AND A PILLOW TO LAY MY HEAD.

OH! AND ONE OTHER THING...

AHA! I KNEW IT!

--A PRIVATE PLACE WHERE I MAY PRAY TO MY GOD.

???

ESTHER'S MODESTY PLEASED HEGAI.

HEGAI GAVE ESTHER THE VERY BEST SPOT IN ALL THE ROOMS TO SLEEP IN, AND 7 MAIDS TO TEND TO HER.

HEGAI PERSONALLY OVERSAW ESTHER'S BEAUTY TREATMENTS AND MADE SURE SHE HAD SPECIAL FOOD TO EAT.

SO FOR MONTHS, EACH YOUNG WOMAN...

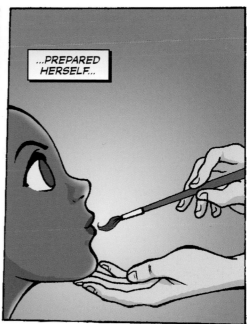

...PREPARED HERSELF...

...AND AWAITED HER TURN...

PLEASE GOD, LET XERXES FIND A QUEEN SOON SO I MAY RETURN HOME...

...TO SEE THE KING.

NO. I DON'T WANT ANY OF THAT.

THIS IS THE KING YOU ARE SEEING, ESTHER!

AND I WILL DO MY BEST TO PLEASE HIM--

--BUT I WILL NOT DO WHAT I KNOW IS WRONG!

LET US GO, THEN-- AND MAY YOUR GOD WATCH OVER YOU!

OF ALL THE GIRLS UNDER MY CARE, YOU ARE EITHER THE MOST FOOLISH...

...OR THE MOST WISE.

WHERE ARE YOUR JEWELS? YOUR MAKE-UP? YOUR FANCY GOWN?

OR ARE YOU MERELY A SERVANT SENT TO PLAY THE LYRE FOR ME?

I AM NOT THE MUSICAL ACCOMPANI-MENT...

RATHER, I AM ESTHER, OH GREAT XERXES.

sniff
sniff
sniff

YOU ARE NOT EVEN WEARING PERFUME...

STRANGE...YOU ARE NOT LIKE THE OTHERS...

THE TIME PASSES...

...AND I CAN SCARCE BELIEVE I SPEND IT JUST LISTENING TO YOU SING...

I ONLY HOPE THAT I PLEASED MY KING...

YOUR NAME IS...

ESTHER, MY KING.

DAYS PASSED, UNTIL FINALLY...

HAVE YOU HEARD?

XERXES HAS MADE HIS CHOICE!

I CAN'T BELIEVE IT! THE DAY IS FINALLY HERE!

I HOPE HE PICKS ME-- I HOPE HE PICKS ME!!!

BONNNG

GATHER AROUND, YOUNG MAIDS...

GREAT XERXES HAS MADE HIS WILL KNOWN!

THANK YOU ALL FOR PARTICIPATING-- WE HAVE SOME LOVELY PARTING GIFTS AND CONSOLATION PRIZES AWAITING YOU...

WHEW!

WAAIIIIIIIIIILLLL!!!

BAM

CRASH

SMASH

TINKLE

FROM THAT MOMENT ON, EVENTS MOVED QUICKLY...

XERXES HAS MADE HIS CHOICE!

HE HAS SELECTED ESTHER AS HIS NEW QUEEN!

HAS HE, NOW?

THEN SHE WILL BE A WIDOW BEFORE THEIR UNION IS SEALED!

THEY'RE PREPARING YOUR COUSIN FOR THE WEDDING.

I DON'T KNOW IF SHE CAN TALK NOW--

WAIT IN THE SHADOWS UNTIL I FIND OUT.

THANK YOU.

XERXES MARRIES THE WENCH TONIGHT!

HAVE YOU THE DAGGERS?

AYE! WE'LL AVENGE QUEEN VASHTI--

--WITH HIS BLOOD!

ASSASSINS! BUT HOW CAN I WARN XERXES? WHO WOULD BELIEVE ME?

ESTHER! YOUR COUSIN HAS SENT A WEDDING PRESENT!

A MISERLY GIFT. HMM... I DON'T RECOGNIZE THAT LANGUAGE...

QUEEN VASHTI'S SERVANTS SEEK TO KILL XERXES

...ER... IT'S A TRADITIONAL WEDDING BLESSING OF MY PEOPLE.

LATER, AT THE WEDDING...

LET US CELEBRATE THIS DAY! PASS OUT MY GIFTS TO MY GUESTS!

ESTHER, IS SOMETHING WRONG?

IF IT PLEASES THE KING, I MUST TALK TO YOU...

ALL I DESIRE IS TO BE A GOOD AND FAITHFUL WIFE.

XERXES LOVED HIS QUEEN ESTHER, AND SHE GREW IN GRACE AND FAVOR IN HIS SIGHT.

BUT JUST AS MORDECAI WARNED, ESTHER DID NOT YET REVEAL TO HIM HER KINDRED NOR HER PEOPLE...

"...my bride, you have thrilled my heart; you have thrilled my heart with a glance of your eyes..."
— Song of Solomon

THIS PRODUCTION IS UNFAIR TO TARANTULA UNION LOCAL 839.

YOU DIDN'T TELL ME SERENITY WAS GOING TO BE ESTHER!

How We Made
"ESTHER, QUEEN OF PERSIA"

by

Serenity Harper (Class 6a)

Too many exclamation points!!!!!!!

I HAD A BEDROOM SCENE WITH DEREK !!!!!

Ha! Stew on THAT, Miss Kimberly Calvin!!!

Derek and I

OK, I know I'm making way too big a thing about it, but still: (Me and Derek) in a bedroom. Yeah, so what if Tim and Eddie and Lori were there with the cameras and stuff and the bedroom was just some painted cardboard and rugs from the thrift shop, I could still pretend it was a real romance.

Too long! This should be several smaller sentences.

Only we didn't do any kissing or anything. Tim said the ancient Persians weren't all smoochy and I said who cares we're making a movie for people today, not a gajillion years ago and Derek said no, let's do it the way Tim wants to do it and that (really really hurt cuz) I knew if K. had been Esther he woulda been all kissy-face but with me it's just sit and pluck your harp and sing a few songs.

really, really hurt because

But still -- I got to be the QUEEN!!! Even if it was only just pretend, I got to be Derek's love interest. Oh, man, if only it could be real! If only, if only...

Oops, better tell ya how we did it so Mr. Pyle won't flunk me: Tim would shoot us against this green screen in different costumes then he would put us into the same picture several times so we looked like a crowd. And the costumes were just crepe paper and bits of cloth and tape but as long as we moved reeeeeal careful they looked cool.

C-ya!

C-ren

P.S. Got to save Derek again! Whee!

We heard the call...

Hey!
Serenity ™
Where did
you go
?!?!?

...and here she is!

Refreshed art!

Restored dialog!

Brand new covers!

Same ol' Serenity!

Don't miss any of her
new re-releases from
Thomas Nelson!
"Bad Girl In Town"
"Stepping Out"
"Basket Case"
"Rave and Rant"
"Snow Biz"
"You Shall Love..."

Find her
=oof!=
in stores
=grunt!=
now!

I sure
hope her
books
aren't
this
heavy!

Don't worry,
they're light
reading...

MAKE THE JUMP TO OUR WEBSITES!

www.SerenityBuzz.com
www.GoofyfootGurl.com
        and
www.RealbuzzStudios.com not only talk about
Serenity and the Prayer Club but also upcoming new
series from Thomas Nelson and Realbuzz Studios like
GOOFYFOOT GURL and many, **many more!**

Make sure you visit us regularly
for advance news, fun facts, downloads, contests
and challenges, as well as online shopping!

Can you make a video?
Do you have a recipe?

Exciting new contests
coming soon to
www.RealbuzzStudios.com!

Looking For

Serenity™ Swag

Or

Goofyfoot™ Gear?

Check out our online shop at
www.RealbuzzStudios.com
www.SerenityBuzz.com
www.GoofyfootGurl.com
www.GoofyfootGuy.com
[Protoypes shown; final product may differ slightly.]

Serenity

Created by Realbuzz Studios, Inc.
Min Kwon, Primary Artist
Alana Yuen, Main Artist

Serenity throws a big wet sloppy one out to:
Joe Bob Briggs -- "The drive-in will never die."

Smack!
Luv Ya !!!

©&TM 2007 by Realbuzz Studios   ISBN 1-59554-396-1 / 978-1-59554-396-7

www.RealbuzzStudios.com
www.SerenityBuzz.com

Published by Thomas Nelson, Inc. Nashville, TN 37214 www.thomasnelson.com

Library of Congress Cataloguing-in-Publication Data
Applied For

Scripture quotations marked NCV are taken from
The Holy Bible, New Century Version®. NCV®.
Copyright © 2001 by Nelson Bibles.
Used by permission of Thomas Nelson. All rights reserved.

Printed in Singapore.
5 4 3 2 1